— DOR
MYSTE~~RIES~~

Introduced by
Jean Stubbs

BOSSINEY BOOKS

First published in 1989 by
Bossiney Books
St Teath, Bodmin, Cornwall

Reprinted 1992

Printed and bound by
Penwell Print Limited
Callington, Cornwall

PLATE ACKNOWLEDGMENTS
Front cover photography by Dorset Media
Services

Back cover photography by Roy Westlake

Ray Bishop: pages 5, 85

Barney Camfield: pages 69, 71, 72, 75,
81, 79,82

BNPA Commercial photography: page 39

John F Sculpher: page 49

Roy Westlake: pages 7, 11, 13, 15, 19,
21, 27, 37, 47, 54, 59, 63

Introducing Dorset Mysteries

Bossiney invites six authors to probe mysterious facets of Dorset. The distinguished novelist Jean Stubbs, who sets the scene for *Dorset Mysteries*, reflects 'This is a strange county, full of strange tales and superstitions . . .'

All writers show us their mysteries are indescribable and various.

Heidi Best considers the career of Isaac Gulliver, King of the Dorset Smugglers. Barney Camfield brings a royal legend to life and finds King Arthur here in Dorset. Jane Langton conjures up the mysterious spirit of Thomas Hardy. Peter Underwood haunts us with unearthly apparitions and Felicity Young examines the extraordinary life and death of Lawrence of Arabia.

'Let us soak you deep in this mysterious, magical place.'

About the author
JEAN STUBBS

Jean Stubbs is the author of sixteen novels. A frequent lecturer at writers' schools and seminars, many of her short stories have been televised or adapted for radio. She lives, with her second husband, in a two-hundred-year-old cottage at Nancegollan near Helston in Cornwall, but has a great affection for Dorset past and present.

Born and brought up in Lancashire, she has lived and worked in Cornwall since 1975 and has contributed two titles to the Bossiney list. In 1985 her first book for Bossiney '100 Years Around the Lizard', was launched at Helston on Flora Day. Then in 1987 she wrote 'Great Houses of Cornwall' in which she toured seven National Trust properties.

Jean Stubbs was the guest speaker at the 1988 Bossiney Literary Lunch held in the Laureate's restaurant – named after Sir John Betjeman – at the St Moritz Hotel, Trebetherick, North Cornwall – in the heart of Betjeman Country.

Jean was one of the first writers in the country to have a micro computer word processor, which she finds invaluable for banking research and editing manuscripts. In 1984 she was appointed Writer in Residence for Avon.

Jean Stubbs

4

The Mystery of Dorset

by Jean Stubbs

In this enchanted region of England known as *The Westcountry,* each county makes a unique contribution to the whole. Cornwall, that wild kingdom beyond the Tamar, keeps itself apart from the rest. Devon dreams a green idyll. Somerset, graced by Glastonbury, exudes a feminine allure. Wiltshire, renowned for its stone circles, is possessed of a stark masculine beauty. But Dorset, the smallest, most lightly-populated and sometimes least-appreciated county of the five, combines the glories of nature with the marvels of man; is as enigmatic as Cornwall, as delectable as Devon, as bewitching as Somerset, as rich in pre-historic monuments as Wiltshire, and adds a final ingredient of its own. Dorset is mysterious.

Mysteries are indescribable and various. There is the mystery of folk memory, so often to be found here. You visit a particular spot, by choice or chance, and unexpectedly feel at one with it. What you experience at that moment you never forget. In times of stress or emptiness you recall it and so renew yourself. You dream, or plan, to return there one day, temporarily or permanently, because this patch of land holds some quality which you can find nowhere else. You believe that you belong there, and in a far-away sense so you do.

Before the industrial revolution people took that feeling of belonging for granted, since the land was part of their existence. And from this they gathered strength and an inner conviction. Nowadays, with most of our population penned in towns and cities, people return to the countryside to find it. Their annual holiday becomes a form of pilgrimage, whether they know it or not, in search of a lost past. In these few brief weeks, hoping to come home as it were, they are seeking a time in which life was lived according to the seasons, nature was served, ancient rituals observed, and old gods propitiated. Do you remember the city businessman, Soames Forsyte of

The Old Mill Pond, Swanage, more than thirty years ago.

Galsworthy's great saga, deciding in old age to find the home of his "Dosset" forebears, and view the land they had once tilled? 'And something moved in him, as if the salty independence of that lonely spot were still in his bones . . . For a moment he seemed to understand even himself.'

Closely linked to this is the magnetism of nature. Compact though it is, Dorset offers an amazing variety of scenery: from the pastoral vales of Blackmoor and the ancient forest of Cranborne Chase in the north; over the great chalk downs which undulate across the county; and down to primeval heathland, quarries of Purbeck marble and Portland stone, the immense harbour at Poole, and an incomparable coastline. Whatever your mood or whim of the moment, Dorset can supply the background to enhance and sustain it.

You are a rambler, a viewer, a consumer of light lunches at country pubs and heavy cream teas at four o'clock sharp, a buyer of orchard-grown fruit at the roadside and fresh eggs from free-ranging hens. There are villages all over the county waiting to entice you, peaceful rustic Edens as yet unacquainted with the serpent of building development, affectionately described by Sir Frederick Treeves in his *Highways & Byways* as having 'no centre, no beginning and no end – merely a casual unarranged sample of rural Dorset'. Their cottages are built of brick and timber or local stone, with roofs intricately thatched or distinctively slated. The church will probably be Norman. A stream runs by or through them. They wear an air of tranquility. Even their names intrigue: 'Ryme Intrinsica, Fontmell Magna, Sturminster Newton and Melbury Bubb,' to quote John Betjeman's first line in his *Dorset* poem. And I also love the sound of Gussage All Saints, Winterborne Stickland, Upsydling, and Purse Caundle whose medieval manor was traditionally supposed to be the hunting lodge of bad King John.

You are a loner, a serious walker, a ponderer of problems and the mystery of life? Roller-coasting across the county, from Wiltshire in the north-east to Somerset and Devon in the South West, are miles of green and pleasant hills, strewn with flints and inhabited only by sheep and their shepherds, a vast calm solitude in which only the wind makes conversation. From their heights you are lord or lady of all you survey, and the views are spell-binding.

You are a delver into past history? The venerable Martyrs' Tree, which still grows in the middle of Tolpuddle, is worth admiring both

The church at Wimborne St Giles – a typical Dorset village.

King Charles II, on his flight across Dorset from Cromwell's soldiers, still found time to grant Godmanstone's smith a licence to sell liquor.

for itself and those it commemorates. Six humble farm labourers banded together beneath the original sycamore to discuss their rights to a wage increase, and were transported to Australia in chains for this hideous crime in 1834. But their plight and punishment roused public sympathy, and though the men suffered the cause flourished.

Would you care to trace the Dorset flight of King Charles II, escaping from Cromwell's soldiers in 1651 after the Battle of Worcester? This is a comical mystery. Apparently he stopped for refreshment at the George Inn, Bridport which no longer exists, and also at a smithy in Godmanstone, because his horse needed shoeing. He asked for refreshment there, too. On hearing that the smith had no licence he granted one on the spot, and from this incident the Smith's Arms was created.

You should certainly visit the engaging village of Corfe, whose castle, café and shop are in the care of the National Trust. If you walk

Picturesque Corfe village dominated by the castle ruins.

around the hill on which Corfe Castle was built you will find a chunk or two lying in the stream below, a side wall bulges mightily, and the front is being restored. Here Edward, King of Wessex and All England, was murdered in 978 AD, and his body first hidden and then thrown down a well. But miracles began to happen. The waters of the well developed healing properties and became a shrine. A blind old woman, in whose cottage the king's corpse had been concealed, found her sight restored by a mystical light. When Edward was declared to be a saint and martyr and his bones rested in Shaftesbury Abbey, she made an annual pilgrimage to his shrine, carrying with her the first flower on which her eyes had opened. And now along her way, from Corfe to Shaftesbury, the white broom grows. Martyr's Broom.

If you are a keen student Wareham is the place for you, with a fine museum. It is a town full of eventful history, first founded by the Early Britons, taken over by the Romans, sacked by the Danes four times in a century and left in ruins, and last captured by the Roundheads. Alfred the Great built his fleet here and gained a naval victory over the Danes in Swanage Bay.

Listen closely. Can you not hear the measured thread of Roman legions marching along the roads they built, from Dorchester to Badbury, from Cranborne Chase to Hamworthy? Can you not hear the measured tones of Roman names in such Dorset towns as Kington Magna, Whitchurch Canicorum, Compton Abbas. Do you sense time passing? Go back, and further back.

For those with eyes to see, a pinch of curiousity to drive them on, and the imagination to make a leaping guess in the dark, pre-historic man has left his messages and riddles in earthworks on the hilltops. According to Colin and Janet Bord in their fascinating book *Mysterious Britain,* these ancient engineers remodelled the landscape so that the earth's natural currents of energy could be strengthened and flow more freely. Then they created sacred enclosures, whose entrances were placed east and west, for the rising and setting of the sun, where pagan priests could conduct solemn rituals and hold joyful ceremonies, and the people danced and sang to arouse beneficial influences.

Looking down on Corfe with its pretty cottages clustered around the church.

In Christian times these powerful rites have dwindled into country festivals and fairs. The all-night celebrations of May Eve are no longer held, but May Day – the first day of the Celtic summer – and Maypole dancing are still popular in rural districts. On midsummer's eve the fires of the summer solstice, originally lit to honour and strengthen the sun, still burn, and prudent folk use particular plants on this witch-ridden night, to protect themselves from evil: rowan, fennel, orpine, vervain, trefoil and rue. And country fairs abound. For centuries a sheep fair was held in September within the prehistoric camp on Woodbury Hill, and is featured by Thomas Hardy in his novel *Far from the Madding Crowd.*

The most breath-taking piece of prehistoric engineering is Maiden Castle, near Dorchester, thought to be some kind of fortress. But, as the Bords say, to defend an area 1,500 feet wide, 3,000 feet long, and 1.5 miles round would demand the services of a quarter of a million soldiers. They believe it to be constructed for ceremonial purposes, probably to worship the Sun, though the name *Maiden* in connection with ancient stones, means *Mother Goddess.* But whatever the reason for its being, to tread the tranquil turf, to gaze from serene heights, to observe the graceful and majestic sculpting of its terraces, is a profound experience.

Badbury Rings, near Wimborne Minster, where two Roman Roads meet, is a marvel of a different and darker sort: an Iron Age camp on a sombre tree-topped hill. The approach to the summit is broad and dignified, and there is a charming toposcope in the centre, but the view is restricted to vistas between clumps of trees, and I found the atmosphere somewhat sinister and claustrophobic. Legend says that King Arthur won his last great victory over the Saxons in the battle of Mons Badonicus nearby, and also received his mortal wound there.

On Giant Hill near Cerne Abbas (the *Abbots Cernel* of Hardy), limned in chalk, is the famous Cerne Abbas Giant, an old inhabitant when Cerne Abbey was built in the fifteenth century, and still carefully preserved though the Abbey is now in ruins. This outsized human representation is credited with powers of fertility which are deeply respected in Dorset. Courting couples tend to avoid him for obvious reasons, but under a new moon barren women have been known to lie on his phallus all night, and married couples have performed the act of love there. Apparently this is not in any sense a fruitless procedure, for even nowadays there are people in the county

14

Dorset's dramatic and uncompromising coast at Seatown near Chideock.

who have the Giant to thank for their existence.

Perhaps the most mysterious thing of all is that earthworks are best seen from the air, built by man as if they were signals to the Gods.

From Gods to fairies, from religion to magic, is only a step, since both are great mysteries. The round barrows of Dorset have been robbed of their kingly corpses, their fine gold and jewels, but all-powerful spirits remain which keep country people at a respectful distance. They say that fairy folk live there now, and if they were disturbed who knows what might happen? And yet there is a homely and rather amusing difference between these and other fairies. The Dorset variety are such chatterboxes that they have been called *Gabbergammies*. Somehow I cannot imagine coming to harm with a gabbergammy.

From fairies to ghosts is merely another step. The most modern one must be Lawrence of Arabia, who was drawn to this mysterious county in search of peace more than half a century ago. He settled in a cottage a few miles north-west of Wareham, called Cloud's Hill, and once said that nothing would take him away from it. According to eye-witnesses he has indeed stayed there, for his elusive shade haunts the cottage, dressed in Arab robes, and on one more prosaic but equally astonishing occasion was seen on a bridge in Wareham wearing RAF uniform. Even the moments before his death are imprinted on the place in which he died in 1935, for as the day dawns many have heard the sound of his motor-cycle roaring at full throttle towards them on its final journey.

Other centuries have left their spirits here and there in the county, castaways on the shore of time. Shadowy ladies glide in blue or grey, or appear in their former homes distinctly visible in every detail. Hooded monks keep silence in death as in life. Vague black figures loom up. As the full moon rises, a coach and horses gallop soundlessly along their old road. A phantom pack of hounds pursue a ghostly quarry. Smells of incense or cigar smoke rise sweetly, powerfully. Unearthly lights flicker. Solitary footsteps pace to and fro, or mount the stairs. And the steady tramp of long-dead feet heralds a ghostly army of Purbeck, marching from Flower's Barrow over Grange Hill.

And the ghosts of another mysterious phenomenon, known as literary inspiration, haunt Dorset. Lyme Regis, an elegant seaside resort whose colour-washed houses and narrow streets tumble headlong down into the harbour, is particularly renowned for its

The Cobb at Lyme Regis. Along this 600-foot length of stone breakwater John Fowles' French Lieutenant's Woman used to walk and wait.

Cobb. This 600-foot length of stone breakwater was first brought to the reading public's attention by Jane Austen, when her heroine Louisa Musgrove slipped and fell from it in *Persuasion*. In 1980 the filming of John Fowles' novel made it known as the outpost of *The French Lieutenant's Woman*.

But Dorset's most famous chronicler is undoubtedly Thomas Hardy, born at Higher Bockhampton, near Dorchester, in 1840. His cottage, a mud and cob structure with a fine thatch, preserved by the National Trust, is immortalised as the Tranter's in *Under the Greenwood Tree*. His imagination has peopled the county with characters, dubbed it with names, woven stories into its fabric, until place and author become one. Should we have known the Great Heath, which is really a series of heaths, quite so well, but for him? For have we not brooded over it with Eustacia Vye, driven along it with the reddleman, worked in it under the blazing summer sun with

17

Clym Yeobright, walked it wearily with his mother, heard a frog flounce in the pond, and seen thirteen glow-worms upon a foxglove leaf light a stone slab for the dice-players?

As befits a writer of national stature, Hardy's ashes lie in Westminster Abbey, but his heart is rightly buried in the thirteenth to fifteenth century church of Stinsford, the *Mellstock* of the novels.

Not all Dorset's sons are such a source of pride. The county has a matchless coastline, rich in secret caves and sly inlets, and at one time abounded with smugglers, led by the infamous but fascinating Isaac Gulliver.

Then there is the lovely mixture of fact and legend, of which Dorset has more than a fair share. Between village and creeks at Poole is a mighty Agglestone (Holy Stone). It is said that when Old Nick was passing by the Isle of Wight one fine day his idle hands picked up this 17-foot high, 400-ton lump of ironstone, and having nothing better to do he light-heartedly aimed the rock at Corfe Castle which was in the process of being built at the time. But fortunately he missed, and as mortal men have not the power of Old Nick's elbow, there it is to this day.

There are local characters, gone but not forgotten. In the churchyard of Worth Matravers is the grave of one Benjamin Jesty, 'an upright and honest man', who 'introduced the Cow Pox by inoculation and who from his great strength of mind made the Experiment from the Cow on his Wife and two Sons in the year 1774'. But not on himself, you will note. This is the first recorded instance of vaccination.

There are the humble famous. Most geological formations can be found in Dorset. Dinosaurs once roamed in Purbeck. And in the fossil-rich blue lias at Charmouth a Victorian carpenter's daughter, 12-year-old Mary Anning, found the saucer-eyed skeleton of Ichtyosaurus in perfect condition.

The coast is worth a long browse in itself. Weymouth would be my choice for a good old-fashioned bucket-and-spade holiday. It still preserves the air and appearance of a highly felicitous Victorian

Weymouth's harbour, tucked around the corner from the main bathing beach, is always a hive of activity.

seaside resort. But natural wonders outweigh natural pleasures. In the constant battle between land and sea astonishing chalk sculptures have been created, such as Durdle Door and Lulworth, whose Cove is shaped like an oyster and lovely as any pearl. Dazzling, turf-topped cliffs lord Lyme Bay, and at Golden Cap reach the highest point on the southern coast. And stretching from St Catherine's Chapel to Portland is one of nature's mysteries: a ten-mile bank of shifting shingle called Chesil Beach. Trudge, slither and crunch your way up this rampart of pebbles, and stand on the top in order to see it spreading out for miles on either side. The pebbles, worn smooth by sea and time, are subtly coloured, and all sizes from marrowfat pea to potato. The holed ones are literally and metaphorically 'holy stones', and sailors would take them to sea as protection against evil. Behind Chesil Beach is the Fleet, a lagoon full of eel-grass which feeds Abbotsbury's celebrated colony of mute swans.

Poking out into the English Channel like the head of a stone bird is the Isle of Portland, which Hardy called *The Gibraltar of Wessex*, and used as a setting for his novel *The Well-beloved*. If you are fortunate enough to visit the pink and white light-house at Portland Bill on a foggy day you will hear the desolate bellow of its foghorn, warning passing ships.

This is a strange county, full of strange tales and superstitions, many of which are explored in this book. Heidi Best considers the career of that rumbustious monarch, Isaac Gulliver, King of the Dorset smugglers. Barney Camfield brings a royal legend to life, and finds King Arthur in the county. Jane Langton conjures up the spirit of Thomas Hardy who, captured by Dorset, recaptured it in prose. Peter Underwood haunts us with those unearthly apparitions who must live some earthly moment over and over again: ghostly gramophone needles stuck on old records. And Felicity Young examines the extraordinary life and death of Lawrence of Arabia.

Let us soak you deep in this mysterious and magical place. Then buy an ordnance survey map, fill the car tank with petrol, pack a stout pair of walking shoes, and discover it again for yourselves.

One of nature's mysteries, the vast shifting shingle bank of Chesil Beach.

About the author
PETER UNDERWOOD

Peter Underwood has been President of the Ghost Club (founded 1862) since 1960 and has probably heard more first-hand ghost stories than any man alive. A long-standing member of The Society for Psychical Research, Vice-President of the Unitarian Society for Psychical Studies, a member of The Folklore Society, The Dracula Society and a former member of the Research Committee of the Psychic Research Organisation, he has lectured, written and broadcast extensively. In 1987 he was elected a Fellow of the Royal Society of Arts.

He took part in the first official investigation into a haunting; has sat with physical and mental mediums, and conducted investigations at seances, been present at exorcisms, experiments at dowsing, precognition, clairvoyance, hypnotism, regression; conducted world-wide tests in telepathy and extrasensory perception, and has personally investigated scores of haunted houses.

Peter Underwood has in all contributed six titles to the Bossiney list, the most recent being 'Mysterious Places' and 'Ghosts of Dorset'.

Peter Underwood.

Haunted Dorset

by Peter Underwood

Dorset hauntings are varied, unpredictable and totally fascinating. What ghosts precisely are is a puzzle which has baffled men and women since the beginning of recorded history. Though ghost stories come to us from all parts of the globe, nobody has yet defined the true nature of ghosts. It is therefore natural and logical to include ghosts in a book of *Dorset Mysteries.*

Ghosts are essentially mysteries and this lovely county of Dorset is, in many ways, a mysterious landscape. Moreover, it is thickly populated by ghostly people and animals – some of whom have become legendary characters like the phantom forms of Judge Jeffreys and Martyn's ape of Athelhampton. There have been reported sightings of Monmouth and Raleigh, murderers and the murdered, nuns and monks, grey ladies, white ladies and black mysterious figures.

In 1988 I had the pleasure of writing Bossiney's first Dorset title: *Ghosts of Dorset.* Now I am happy to contribute a chapter to this, their third Dorset publication. This time, dealing with Dorset's phantom population, I turn the spotlight on some of the ghosts that, perhaps appropriately, have never before seen the light of publication – the lesser known ghosts of the county.

We have not yet discovered a way of proving the existence of ghosts, but the wealth and variety of Dorset's ghosts is impressive.

It is interesting to realise that there are more reported ghosts of nuns and monks than any other category of mankind and some might think that these good souls should surely rest in peace if any of us should. But perhaps that is not really the point for I have long been convinced that concentrated thought has something to do with some

A Cavalier is said to haunt the premises of The Pedlar Restaurant at Bridport.

24

ghostly manifestations; after all there are more reportedly haunted churches than any other type of building and more haunted rectories and vicarages than any other type of inhabited building. Generalising on ghosts however, is a futile occupation for there are always exceptions to any criteria for ghostly appearances; far more important I feel is the objective and careful first-hand reporting of spontaneous cases as they occur. So let us take a brief look at some of the less well-known ghostly happenings in Dorset.

✳   ✳   ✳

Spending a few hours in Bridport in June, 1988, my wife and I chanced to have a cup of coffee in The Pedlar Restaurant and I caught sight of a framed photograph purporting to depict the ghost that reputedly haunts the premises.

I learned that the photograph was taken during the refurbishment and, in part, the re-building of the old Water Mill there in 1984. The lower floor of the premises had once been a museum and the vicinity of the mill wheel had, it was said, been the scene of a number of apparently paranormal incidents.

The photograph, which seemed to me to be very indistinct and obviously the subject of some kind of light interference, was said to show a cavalier, circa 1629, and a lady with a naked child clinging to her. She seems to be pointing past the cavalier who is facing her.

On two occasions, it is said, before the photograph was acquired, the ghostly form of a cavalier – without the lady and the child – was seen by one of the present owner, Alan Morton's, family. The same form was, according to Mr Morton, seen by an electrician working on the renovations.

I have been unable to obtain any further information, confirmatory or otherwise, but the photograph is certainly interesting and if it depicts a ghost figure previously seen in the vicinity, then that is all the more interesting. At all events they serve a good cup of coffee at The Pedlar!

✳   ✳   ✳

On the same occasion I made a point of meeting John Sales, the local historian and curator of Bridport Museum and an Honorary Townsman of Bridport. He was kind enough to find time to tell me something of the history and some of the curious happenings

Bridport's museum, one of the town's oldest properties, exudes a 'curious atmosphere.'

The Castle, South Street, where Bridport's museum is housed, dates back to the sixteenth century. Felicity Young's drawing is based on an old print dating from the 1860s.

reportedly experienced in two of Bridport's oldest properties, the museum itself and the nearby Chantry.

The building in which Bridport Museum is now housed dates back to the early sixteenth century and is of two storeys. Although the exact purpose of the original building is now unknown, it seems to have long been referred to as a castle, possibly due to its appearance, possibly because of its close proximity to the tenement of Castlehay. It may have once been the house of a priest of some standing – on the first floor there is a corbel carved with a half-angel holding a book – and certainly over the years it has served as an inn, The Old Castle Inn; as a penny savings bank; as a meeting place for working men and for the Oddfellows and the Conservative Club. It was presented to the town in 1932 for use as a museum and art gallery.

Mr Sales said that several visitors had remarked upon a 'curious atmosphere' in the upper part of the old building. One couple in particular went upstairs but the wife returned almost immediately saying she had encountered a very malevolent 'something' up there and she could not stay in the building a moment longer. Shortly afterwards her husband also came downstairs and said he too had distinctly felt an 'unwelcome atmosphere' up there and they both said the place was extremely haunted.

Some time later another visitor also said the upper storey was haunted. And she pointed out the same spot as that indicated by the previous couple as the place which exuded a definite feeling of something not of this world – although she thought that the influence was in the main beneficial and, she thought, a kindly apparition haunted the place!

The other, equally old, building in Bridport that interested me was The Chantry which, curiously enough, had also long had the name 'Castle' attached to it. Here again it may be that the appearance of the building caused it to be so-called although documentary research has clearly established that it had once been a chantry as its current name implies. Here again the original purpose of the building is obscure but it could well date from as early as the thirteenth century and might have once been a guardhouse. Indeed the sturdy nature of the building supports the idea that it was used as a dungeon for criminals or as a local gaol. The upper storey gives a good view across to the harbour and a series of projecting stones located high up on the south wall appear to be the mounting for a cresset or beacon so that the building could well also have acted as a primitive lighthouse or watchtower.

The discovery of a priests' columbarium or pigeon loft in the attic and the shape and position of the corbels supporting the first floor all suggest that part of the premises was once used to celebrate Mass. Also the presence of a piscina opposite the doorway also points to the use of the premises as a chantry which would have come to an end in the early sixteenth century after the dissolution of the religious houses. The building then became a private residence and so remained until 1972.

Here too a number of visitors have reported strange feelings and stranger happenings. Once a lady borrowed the keys saying she was interested in the empty building and would love to have a look round. She soon returned saying the place was 'terribly haunted' and said she was sure that a great amount of cruelty had taken place there, even murder. There were 'unquiet spirits' roaming about the seemingly empty building. 'Oh yes, terribly haunted,' she said and nothing would induce her ever to enter the place again.

Intrigued by all this John Sales decided to spend some hours of darkness in the building alone, which he did and although he told me he stayed there very late, he neither heard nor saw anything he could not adequately explain. Yet, shortly afterwards, another visitor expressed interest in The Chantry and John loaned her the key, curious to know what she would make of it.

He began to get worried when hours passed and she had not returned but, just as the museum was closing, return she did and said she really thought the place was haunted – but by such a sweet and kindly spirit that she was reluctant to leave the building.

When the couple who were so distressed in the museum asked John whether he had not noticed the atmosphere in the top part of the building, and he replied 'No', they were most surprised and said he must be 'very insensitive' – which I find difficult to believe. But sensitivity and being aware of something outside and beyond this world of ours is not a gift that is bestowed upon all of us.

*   *   *

The prosaic premises of 'Two Counties Radio' studios in Southcote Road, Bournemouth, may even be haunted. One of the resident presenters, Tim Butcher, was working in the studio one night, he told me, and he was the only person in the studios at the time, when he saw reflected in the glass behind him the unmistakable figure of a stocky, thick-set man standing with his back to the wall of Studio One. Tim turned at once but there was no one there.

Another time when the caretaker was alone in the building he heard and saw a window with louvre-type shutters, shaking and rattling. Thinking that a window must have been left open, he went into the room. There was no open window and the shutter was still while he was in the room. Satisfied that all was well he left the room; as he closed the door behind him he thought he heard something and looking round he saw the shutter rattling and shaking again.

There have been other strange happenings too but the presence, if presence there is, seems harmless enough and no one is too worried. But Tim Butcher tells me he is totally convinced that he saw something quite inexplicable and the caretaker is an equally convincing witness.

*　　　*　　　*

The beautiful, rambling and romantic Tudor Wolfeton Manor with its medieval gatehouse and even older unmatched towers is the home of Captain and Mrs N.T.L. Thimbleby and they live in peace with the ghosts that haunt their home just outside Dorchester.

For centuries the property belonged to the Trenchard family, until in fact the early part of the last century, and a member of this ancient family is said to have won a wager by driving a coach and horses up the great main stairway with its vaulted and arched ceiling and strange figures looking down. It is reputed that on occasions this remarkable feat is repeated by a ghostly coach and horses.

Apart from the stairway and the great hall, Wolfeton's glories include a chapel, a cider house, a parlour and a haunted dining room. The latter is furnished and the table set as it must have been long years ago when a curious event occured, an event that makes Wolfeton unique in the annals of psychical phenomena.

It happened during the ownership of Sir Thomas Trenchard (1630-57), an assize judge and a man of considerable standing and reliability. One evening he, his family and guests had just sat down to dine when suddenly the sober Sir Thomas looked towards his wife, seated at the other end of the great refectory table, and he seemed to be shocked to the core for a moment. Then, to everyone's surprise, he ordered his carriage to be made ready and abruptly, without a word of

The beautiful, rambling and romantic Wolfeton Manor where phantoms linger.

explanation, he left his wife, guests and the house and set out in his carriage accompanied by his marshal whom he had summoned.

On the way to Dorchester he related to his marshal, seated beside him, the reason for his sudden and untimely departure from Wolfeton. He said he had distinctly seen, standing behind Lady Trenchard's chair, a double of her Ladyship but the awful thing was that the standing figure had its own head under one arm and the blood poured down from the slashed neck.

Before the marshal had time to reassure Sir Thomas Trenchard that he must have been imagining things, a messenger on horseback from Wolfeton House overtook the carriage, signalling wildly that he had news for Sir Thomas. The coach came to a halt and the messenger blurted out the news that Lady Trenchard had just committed suicide by cutting her throat. Her ghost, headless and dressed in grey, still haunts the house and has been seen in the dining room and in the room where the deed presumably took place.

There is another ghost that has been seen at Wolfeton, from another period of time and recalling another tragic, ghastly historical happening. A phantom Catholic priest haunts the atmospheric gatehouse where he was once held prisoner. He was taken from there to Dorchester, where he was hung, drawn and quartered. Small wonder that something of the last unquiet days of his tormented spirit lingers to this day at haunted Wolfeton.

Dorset is indeed a county shrouded in mystery.

Lulworth Cove is a magic place and many are the stories and legends associated with this almost land-locked bay and the immediate area which includes the forty-foot rock arch of Durdle Door, the chasm of Stair Hole, the rocks of Worbarrow Bay and the village of East Lulworth with its thatched cottages and shell of the sixteenth century castle, gutted by fire in 1929.

The phantom form of Napoleon himself has been seen on the beach at Lulworth Cove; the unmistakable form is seen with a companion, seemingly looking for a suitable landing-place for an invasion of England. After a moment, he turns dejectedly away, folds his maps – and disappears. In 1930 one witness told her story of seeing the forms as they had occasionally been seen for many years and fifty years later a visitor told me he, too, had seen the same ghostly appearance. At the time he had no knowledge of the story and thought at first he was seeing the rehearsal for a film or television performance, until the two figures walked towards the sea and completely disappeared. The first sighting of this odd spectacle seems to have been around 1804. Thomas Hardy thought he had invented the idea of Napoleon landing at Lulworth for the purpose of a short story in 1882 and was astonished when friends told him they knew of such a tradition and that the ghost of Napoleon had in fact been seen in the cove.

When fire destroyed Lulworth Castle, the magnificent home of the Weld family, in 1929 there was much speculation as to the fate of twelve maidservants at the castle for they all completely disappeared – possibly they left the area when the castle and their possessions went up in flames and stayed quiet for the rest of their lives; possibly, or perhaps there was some sinister or tragic aspect to their disappearance for they were certainly never seen or heard of again. There was a story at the time that all twelve had walked along the cliff path to Durdle Door and had been washed into the sea and perished without anyone hearing their screams for help.

Such an occurrence could explain the experience of a former naval commander and others who have heard screams of frantic

The phantom form of Napoleon himself has been seen on the beach at Lulworth Cove.

Speculation still surrounds the fate of twelve maidservants from Lulworth Castle who, when fire gutted the castle in 1929, were said to have walked along the cliff path to Durdle Door and perished in the sea.

females off Lulworth Cove late at night. The commander never forgot the night, some fifty years ago now, when his ship was anchored off Lulworth. He was in his cabin and it was getting late when he thought he heard a 'wild crescendo of screams' and he hurried up the companion-way, his heart in his mouth. Desperately he sought to pierce the seemingly solid wall of blackness, towards the north where the frightful sounds seemed to originate but he could see nothing. Still the blood-curdling screams came wafting towards him, loud and clear one moment, fading and far away the next. Then the screaming ceased, 'as abruptly as if the dark waters had quenched it'. He turned towards the beach and there he thought he could see something; yes, he could just distinguish a figure on the foreshore, a young girl. As he watched, the figure seemed to jerk awkwardly and began what looked like a macabre kind of dance; another figure joined her and another and another. Soon there seemed to be ten or a dozen girls prancing and jumping about the shore in total silence. The Commander watched for several moments – or so it seemed, perhaps it was only seconds – and then, suddenly, the figures stopped moving and were completely still and motionless, almost as if they had been switched off. Then he realised that the forms were growing fainter and soon they had completely disappeared. The foreshore was empty and deserted. Had he seen the ghosts of the drowned maidservants of Lulworth Castle? Other people have reported similar sights and scenes and screams in this strange place.

Lulworth Cove is also the haunt of a ghostly black dog and nearby there is the ghost of a girl who committed suicide and was buried without a coffin, with a stake through her heart. And phantom marching men have been heard and seen on Bindon Hill – these are just a few of Dorset's spectral population.

Lulworth Cove, the haunt of many a spectre.

About the author
HEIDI BEST

Heidi Best is editor of 'Somerset & Avon Life' magazine, and lives in Somerset. She is the author of Blandford's 'How To Book of Horses and Riding' and has contributed to a variety of books and magazines, including many articles on Dorset.

Born in Surrey, Heidi Best moved to the Westcountry in 1979 after visiting farming friends in Somerset and deciding that she would like to live there when she retired. On second thoughts, she resolved not to wait for retirement – which was 40 years ahead – and left her job as assistant editor on two national magazines, 'Pony' and 'Light Horse', to freelance in Somerset before taking up her post with 'Somerset & Avon Life' in 1983. She has received critical acclaim for her features on personalities as diverse as Roald Dahl, Auberon Waugh, Jeffrey Archer, Nigel Dempster and Jane Seymour among others, as well as for her articles on environmental issues affecting the area.

Heidi Best.

The King of Dorset Smugglers

by *Heidi Best*

It is a dark, moonless night, bombazine black. The howl of a distant dog, and a cow bellowing to her calf, can be heard above the breeze that gently stirs the leaves on the trees. In the village the cottagers sleep, though some beds are empty. Those safely behind closed doors, blankets pulled to their chins, sleep fitfully, knowing that something is afoot in the bay across the moors; aroused from uneasy slumber, they hear the sound of muffled feet and hooves on cobbles and the creak of turning wagon wheels barely discernible in the deserted dark outside their doors, as the band of men and horses move through the streets, across the heather-clad moor to Bourn Mouth, a desolate spot.

In the bay the dark form of a ship can just be made out against the inky skyline. The sails are furled, and the squeak of ropes can be heard as men go quietly yet speedily about their tasks. Casks of brandy, bolts of lace and silk – the cutter has come from France, laden with luxuries for the over-taxed English. The contraband is loaded into rowing boats. Strong-armed men lift and stack, wipe their brows with brightly coloured kerchiefs, then return to their labours. As each boat takes on a full load, the strong arms turn to rowing and there are helping hands to beach each craft on the sand as it comes to land.

A carter stands with his horse while the booty is loaded. The cob snorts and the carter's hand flies to cover its nostrils. On the dunes above, a horse flicks its ears in response to the snort, but remains silent. Its rider, clothed in black and wearing a powdered wig beneath his tricorn hat, is careful to avoid being silhouetted against the skyline as he keeps watch for the preventive men. The smugglers are in luck. The preventive men, busy further along the coast, do not appear, and the haul is taken across the moor and stored in safe cellars in the village before dawn streaks the sky. Sighs of relief greet the men who creep back into their cottages before first light, and

Dorset's cliffs drop sheer into the English Channel as it pounds and sucks relentlessly at their base.

climb into bed to grab a few hours' sleep. The horses, sacking mufflers removed from around their hooves, eat their hay and doze. Another night is over; another illicit haul safely stored, and no blood shed – this time.

The events described were typical of many a dark night on England's coasts, particularly during the eighteenth century. Smuggling reached a pinnacle during and just after the Napoleonic Wars, and much of the activity took place on Dorset's deserted coastline. Few who could afford to buy smuggled goods said nay to an opportunity to purchase luxury items made prohibitively expensive by the high import duties levied upon them by the government of the time.

Some measure of the size of the illegal trade is shown by the

41

amounts of some of the smuggled goods seized in 1822, 1823 and 1824 by government agents – 227,000 gallons of gin, 902,684 pounds of tobacco, 3,000 pounds of snuff – remembering that these figures show only a fraction of the goods that actually reached England's shores. Tea, brandy, wines, lace, silks, fine cottons and linens – there was no shortage of people who desired to enrich their lives with these luxury products, and no shortage of daring and sometimes desperate men who would risk all to defy the duty men and bring such goods across the English Channel.

They were villains, of course. Some were cut-throats, like the unscrupulous Robert Kingsmill, leader of the cruel, tyrannic, callous killers known as the Hawkhurst Gang, of Kent. But Isaac Gulliver, well-known throughout Dorset and Hampshire, prepossessing, sophisticated, gentlemanly and popular, was of a different stamp altogether.

Born in the Wiltshire village of Seamington on September 5, 1745, little is known of the childhood of the man who was to become a legend in south coast counties for his smuggling activities and audacity. We do know that at the age of 23 he was married in 1768 at Sixpenny Handley parish church, to Elizabeth Beale. Five years older than him, Elizabeth may have been the daughter of William Beale, owner of the Blacksmith's Arms at Thorney Down, an inn which was taken over by Gulliver who changed its name to the King's Arms. Though he was undoubtedly a rogue, Isaac Gulliver's sophistication contributed in no small way to romanticising the trade in which he was involved.

Since all levels of society gained from smuggling, from the smugglers themselves to lords and ladies, the authorities found it nigh on impossible to stamp out the trade that brought such benefits to most in the community. Theirs was an uphill struggle, and as the rate of duty payable increased over the years, smuggling became even more profitable, involving men from all professions to the point where there were very few who would lend a hand to the preventive men as they struggled to apprehend the popular villains.

When the authorities were successful, fines were imposed upon the guilty, who were imprisoned until the monies could be paid. Dorchester gaol's calendar of prisoners from 1800 to 1821 lists 69 men and one woman convicted for smuggling. The same names appear time and time again, proving that imprisonment was no deterrent to the folk who aided and abetted, or were members of, one or another of

Sixpenny Handley Church where the audacious Isaac Gulliver married his bride Elizabeth Beale, the innkeeper's daughter.

the gangs. Goods collected when the guilty were apprehended were put up for auction; in March 1778, for instance, at the Custom House in Lyme Regis, 130 gallons of rum, 325 of brandy, 105 of Geneva, 40 pounds of coffee beans, 4,509 pounds of Bohea tea and 22 pounds of green tea, were offered for auction.

Smart Isaac Gulliver was never caught, though it was obvious to anybody who could put two and two together and come up with four that where he happened to be, strange events took place. When he was 33 he moved to Longham and made it his headquarters, letting the King's Arms at Thorney Down to a tenant, but no sooner had he left Thorney Down that the preventive men confiscated some smuggled spirits and tea nearby. A large gang of smugglers armed with pistols and cutlasses rode into Blandford that evening, reclaiming their goods from the preventive officer's house and galloping off, cowboy-style, firing their pistols into the air and flinging two kegs of spirits to the enthralled crowd as a gesture of goodwill.

A year later there was more activity at Thorney Down when six dragoons searching for contraband in Hook's Wood were met by more than 40 smugglers who, once again, reclaimed the goods before beating the dragoons and stealing their horses. Was Isaac Gulliver connected with these two events? We shall probably never know, but the likelihood seems high in view of future activities. The clever, outwardly respectable, prosperous businessman was ideally placed at Longham to mastermind such schemes. Evidence against him, however, was little.

Evidence might have been in short supply, but tales of derring-do and barefaced cheek revolving around Isaac Gulliver and his 50 or so loyal, uniformed men – complete with powdered hair and known as 'The White Wigs' – were legion. Once, when Gulliver was visited at his home by preventive men, he fooled them, far-fetched as it may sound, by putting white chalk on his face and lying in a coffin. One cannot help thinking that preventive men foolish enough to fall for such a ruse rather deserved to fail in their quest. It makes the story of him being carried through the streets of Poole in a barrel, or escaping by being disguised as a shepherd, seem very tame by comparison.

Perhaps it was an act of desperation that caused the Government to announce in 1782 that it would bestow a free pardon upon any smuggler who would atone for his sins by serving in the Navy – or find a substitute to serve for him. Surprisingly, since Navy life was tough and dangerous, it was not difficult to find such substitutes for the quite large sums of money that affluent smugglers could afford. Gulliver chose to wipe his slate clean and took the latter course of action, leaving Longham and moving his family to Devon, where he took up the reins of his former trade as a wine and spirit merchant.

Once a rogue, always a rogue; though his outward façade of respectability had many fooled, he could not mend his ways and soon controlled a smuggling operation which stretched the considerable distance from Torbay to Lymington, a coastline which, with its prevailing southwesterly wind, gave a fast sea passage, and whose rich mixture of sandy beaches, coves and chines, deserted moorlands and heavy woods, favoured the illicit trade and hampered the activities of the authorities. And, naturally, corruption among the

44

preventive men was not unknown.

Adding to the story of Gulliver's pardon in 1782 is the tale which purports that it was not of the standard variety offered to other smugglers, but a special pardon by King George III – who popularised Weymouth and the surrounding area. Clever Gulliver had discovered a French plot to assassinate the king, whose thanks subsequently also took the form of royal permission to smuggle whenever Gulliver felt so inclined. Smuggler by royal appointment?

So great was Gulliver's fame that before the pardon was mooted, His Majesty's Commissioners of Customs in London asked the Poole customs officers – to whom, infuriatingly for them, Gulliver was known at that time as the greatest and most notorious smuggler in the West of England – for a report on the elusive thief. As usual, though, there was no proof to be had.

The name of Gulliver is, of course, synonymous with the intrepid traveller who happened upon Lilliput, and it is said that the neighbourhood bearing that name was probably so dubbed because those who lived there compared their hero with the eponymous fictitious character. Isaac Gulliver probably did live at Flag Farm in Lilliput for a period, and without doubt the area would have been well suited to his trade.

But even seemingly immortal heroes who elude the forces of law and order with dexterity are eventually caught by time. The wealthy, respected, landowning citizen who had amassed vast wealth by nefarious activities, albeit without violence or bloodshed, eventually settled, a pillar of society, in Wimborne, marrying his daughter to a local banker.

Unlucky for some, and so it was for him, Friday, September 13, 1822, was the day on which Isaac Gulliver died. He played the preventive men on a string as a cat plays with a mouse, amassed vast wealth for himself, employed many men and women, and brought to the people of the West and South those luxury goods which they demanded in such volume, at a price they could afford. Though he was dishonest, in an age when violence was rife, he achieved his ends without resorting to it himself, thus becoming the perfect example of the gentleman smuggler described affectionately by Charles Lamb as 'the only honest thief.' In modern times, smugglers have switched in many cases from luxury goods to drugs – or even people – and the image of the honest thief has gone forever.

Gulliver's grave lies under the centre aisle in Wimborne Minster

Church of St Cuthburga, a building which then, as now, dominates the town. His death was noted in the *Gentleman's Magazine* and the *Salisbury and Winchester Journal.*

There are other landmarks throughout Dorset which mark the exploits of the man who might claim to be the king of Dorset smugglers. The Decoy Pond at Westbourne was a secret meeting place for smugglers: Gulliver is reported to have hidden his illicitly transported goods in a well at Branksome Chine, the remains of which may still be viewed from near Seaward Path.

Kinson parish church, not far from Longham, was a hive of smuggling and poaching activity; the large tower gave excellent storage space, and within living memory it was possible to see the grooves in the sides of the tower made by the ropes with which the audacious and irreverent smugglers hauled up their goods for safe keeping. Accustomed as they were to working at dead of night, in lonely locations, it obviously troubled the smugglers not a jot when they used a tomb in the churchyard as an alternative hiding place; whereas the tower would be a likely spot for the preventive men to search, no doubt they were far less inclined to feel like opening a grave, making such a hiding place ideal for extra-precious goods.

As befits the legend surrounding this king of Dorset smugglers, it is said that Gulliver's last operation involved three ships landing cargoes near to the spot where Bournemouth pier now stretches into the sea. The lonely, heather-clad heath, out of bounds at dead of night to all but the stoutest hearts, witnessed an incredible two-mile convoy of pack ponies led, on this instance, by the dashing smuggler himself, Isaac Gulliver, who led a double life – that of gentleman and roguish lawbreaker, and thus ensured himself an affectionate spot in the history of that great eighteenth century activity – smuggling.

Bournemouth's vast expanse of beach where now holidaymakers take the air. But when Gulliver mounted his last operation in the eighteenth century witnesses watched an incredible two-mile convoy of pack ponies led along these cliffs.

About the author
JANE LANGTON

Jane Langton, who lives in Torquay, is a member of an old established Devon family whose roots go back to the seventeenth century. Jane was for several years a well-known voice and skilful interviewer in local radio, but in 1988 she moved into the field of Westcountry newspapers. Married to John Reynolds, a senior presenter at DevonAir, she loves wind-surfing and is often to be found in Lyme Bay. A Capricorn subject, she aims to devote more time to writing. Of her chapter on 'The Magic and Mystery of Thomas Hardy' she says: 'It's not yet another critical appreciation of the genius of Hardy, more an exploration into the reasons for his worldwide fascination. I write as an admirer, not a critic.' Jane is currently working on 'Devon Curiosities', an intriguing illustrated tour of Devon, which Bossiney will publish later in 1989.

Jane Langton
Photo: John F. Sculpher, Exeter

The Magic and Mystery of Thomas Hardy

by Jane Langton

Thomas Hardy is arguably Dorset's most famous son.

Should you travel around the county looking for places named in his books you will find them; such is the power of Hardy's description. His beloved Wessex becomes reality. His heroes and heroines haunt the landscape and seem more alive than many real men and women in history. A healthy tourist industry has grown up around this remarkable man.

Hardy, to this day though, remains an enigmatic character while his works fascinate and charm readers worldwide. They are the people who travel to Dorset to try and unlock the mystery.

But then the profession of an author is in itself a mysterious process. Where do the thoughts, the inspiration come from? In that split second between committing a word to paper, either by pen as in Hardy's case, or by the word processors of today, what changes might an author make? Writing is a baffling, multi-faceted process. For great authors like Hardy, it is a gift, a talent to enchant and enthrall the reader; 'supernatural' in the true sense of the word. Surely when we fully understand the nature of this magical part of life we will have found the key to a great mystery, but will lose a valuable, whimsical quality. Hardy's mystery however, is intact and long may it remain so.

Hardy was born on June 2, 1840 at Higher Bockhampton, a hamlet just outside of Dorchester where his father Thomas, a stonemason and mother, Jemima, owned a small cottage. It was on the edge of Egdon Heath, which Hardy was later to describe as picturesque with

The statue in Dorchester commemorates one of English literature's great men.

'trees, clipped hedges, orchards, white gatepost-balls'. An avenue of cherry trees led to their home. The family were well established in the area and Hardy knew more about his ancestors than most people through his grandmother, who lived with them, and his mother. Both had an impressive knowledge of local traditions – Hardy's grandmother would recount to him how she heard the news of the French Revolution. Of his mother he once said she was: ' . . . a girl of unusual ability and judgement', and may have inspired the character of Mrs Yeobright in *The Return of The Native.*

Thomas, himself, would later recall memories of men in stocks, of Corn Law agitation – the Corn Laws were repealed in 1846 when he was six – and of public hangings. Many of these he incorporated into his novels along with hiring fairs – in *Far From the Madding Crowd* and *The Mayor of Casterbridge* – and child labour in *Jude The Obscure* which reflected the social conditions of the time.

He was a quiet, introverted child. In fact he nearly did not make it into the world as he was thought to be dead at birth and was thrown

Hardy's Dorset has changed little in many places.

aside while the doctor attended to his mother. Luckily a nurse noticed him breathing and his life was saved. When grown he was only 5 feet 7 inches tall and several years later, Robert Louis Stevenson's American wife was to write to her mother-in-law '. . . we saw Hardy the novelist at Dorchester . . . a pale, gentle, frightened little man, that one felt an instinctive tenderness for . . .' A child who loved his own company, loved nature, had excellent hearing and could distinguish the different bird songs in the dawn! He loved music too and revelled in playing his violin along with his father and uncle at churches, weddings and other local social occasions.

On leaving school he was apprenticed to a local architect, John Hicks, who encouraged him to continue reading as his mother had done, to widen his education. Hardy was always aware of his simple origins compared to some of the people he later met in London society. Indeed, it was a subject that his first wife Emma constantly raised in comparing her relatively middle-class background – she was the daughter of a Plymouth solicitor – to his.

In 1862 he moved to London to work as an assistant architect and lived there for five years, soaking up the vast quantities of culture available to him in museums, theatres and exhibitions. He came to know London well and it rankled with him that reviewers of his novels would later pigeon-hole him as a simple, provincial novelist. He commented that he knew every street and alley west of St Paul's like a born Londoner, which he was often supposed to be.

In London he once had the curious task of supervising the digging of cuttings for the proposed Midland Railway through the old St Pancras churchyard. Like many Victorians he had a morbid fascination for death and listened eagerly to the gruesome stories of the workers while they transported the bones to other burial places!

Returning to Dorset in 1867 he embarked on his first novel, *The Poor Man and The Lady* which was never published. Three years later he met Emma Gifford on a business trip to St Juliot in Cornwall, the woman who was to become the first Mrs Hardy. Emma had her faults but during their four year courtship she encouraged him to continue with his writing and it is largely due to her support, and that received from his close friend Horace Moule, that Hardy stuck with it. Hardy

Hardy's birthplace at Higher Bockhampton.

The charming village of Abbotsbury.

often had periods of depression during his life, feeling he had not accomplished very much. In November 1927 his second wife Florence noted: 'Speaking about ambition T. said today that he had done all that he meant to do, but did not know whether it had been worth doing.'

As a child Hardy confessed to his mother that he did not want to grow up and in the poem *Childhood Among The Ferns* pictured himself lying on a rainy day in the shelter of a house of ferns: 'Why should I have to grow to man's estate.'

In 1871 his first book appeared, *Desperate Remedies* which Hardy himself paid to be published. And though not a great success, it was

Thomas Hardy.

followed by *Under The Greenwood Tree, A Pair of Blue Eyes* and then the novel that was to bring him recognition, *Far From The Madding Crowd.* The same year that it appeared, 1874, Hardy married Emma and they spent the next ten years living in Dorset, Somerset and London until finally settling at Max Gate, a house that Hardy himself designed and his brother Henry built just on the edge of Dorchester.

This was where he was to live for the rest of his life apart from his travels, where he wrote his greatest novels, and, after the last novel *Jude The Obscure* – published in 1895 – wrote his prodigious poetry. Many people know Hardy as a novelist but in addition to the fourteen novels he wrote over 900 poems plus some 40 short stories and two verse dramas.

It seems strange that this man who achieved such success and recognition during his own lifetime – he was honoured with degrees from Oxford, Cambridge, Aberdeen and Bristol Universities plus the Order Of Merit in 1910 – could write literature that seems quite

Hangman's Cottage, Dorchester, a 1917 picture postcard.

melancholy in tone. It deals with human tragedy, passion, disillusionment and despair. Perhaps it is because in his own life he felt all of these emotions but kept them hidden beneath a public face.

Hardy had a modest attitude to his work simply hoping he would be a 'good hand at a serial', and though he became better at ignoring criticism in later life he hated to hear adverse reviews.

Much has been written about Hardy's relationship with his first wife Emma; the early bloom of love turning to estrangement after a few short years, then the astonishment of his contemporaries when, after her death in 1912 he seemed to never finish mourning her passing by writing some of his greatest love poems in her memory. There are indeed 40 autobiographical poems in which his Cornish romance is enshrined. One is called *A Two Year's Idyll* describing the relationship as: 'A Preface without any book, A Trumpet uplipped, but no call.'

It was as if once they were parted Emma could arouse more emotion in him than at any other time. He even took the second Mrs Hardy, Florence – whom he married in 1914 – on pilgrimages to

Cornwall where he took great pleasure in recalling to her the years of courtship 40 years earlier. He wrote 'it was quite natural: one looked back through the years and saw some pictures: a loss like that makes one's old brain vocal!'

Florence bore these trips remarkably well. And to her credit she brought an order into Hardy's later years, enabling him to continue writing and their fourteen year marriage was essentially a happy one. Hardy died on January 11, 1928, his last volume of poetry was published posthumously later the same year and his biography, which he had written himself was left for Florence to publish under her own name. The mystery of Hardy the man may well stem from the fact that it was Hardy himself who took charge of his memorial by making copious notes on his life.

From the style of the biography it is easy to tell that Florence did not write it herself, though she, of course, added notes she had made in her own diary. She wrote to a friend in 1916 'I keep a diary . . . but

A monument to Thomas Hardy stands outside his birthplace at Higher Bockhampton.

when I remember the awful diary the first Mrs T. H. kept – which Thomas burned – full of venom, hatred and abuse of him and his family, I am afraid to do more than chronicle facts.' Indeed, Hardy destroyed many of his other papers too. In 1919 he wrote to a friend 'I have not been doing much – mainly destroying papers of the last thirty or forty years.'

Although his *Life* gives the reader an insight into the man can any human being be trusted to be totally truthful and objective about themselves, even a man of such genius as Hardy? The novelist Anthony Trollope once said 'no-one could bear to tell the truth about himself.'

Nor did Hardy see letters as an extension of his literary genius. Around 70 of his letters to Emma, mostly written in the latter part of their relationship, have been collected but he never made any effort to be intimate or charming or graceful. Emma's letters have not survived. That is a shame, because contemporary letters are facts and are not open to the interpretation of motives by biographers, there is no room for conjecture. So we have mystery surrounding his personal recorded life, we are to see only what Hardy intended. There is little doubt that he was an enigmatic figure. He lived quite separate lives publicly and privately.

Publicly he enjoyed his trips to London. In 1893 he had met Florence Henniker, a society hostess on a trip to Dublin. He secretly admired her and they found many things in common including a love of literature. It was through this relationship that Hardy met all sorts of people; politicians, other novelists of the day such as H. Rider Haggard, Kipling, Lord Randolph Churchill, Sir Redvers Buller. In addition, his literary fame had enabled membership of two clubs in London, The Savile and The Athenaeum where he rubbed shoulders again with the 'Who's Who' in London society. Theatre visits, lunches and 'crushes', as he called large social gatherings, were enjoyed by Emma too, but in their later years together it was usually Hardy who went alone.

However, he was always glad to return to his beloved Dorset especially when the weather became too hot for the city: 'that hot plate of humanity, on which we first sing, then simmer, then boil, then dry away to dust and ashes.'

In addition to his trips to London to catch up with the latest gossip the Hardys entertained at home at Max Gate. Emma increasingly apologised for her husband's outspoken views and

Thatched cottages at Burton Bradstock.

The view from Hardy's cottage.

would remind Hardy that she was the accomplished one with social graces. T.P. O'Connor gives an account of Mrs Hardy's conduct after she felt her husband too rude, too honest when asked of an opinion. O'Connor quotes Mrs Hardy thus: 'You know, he's very vain and very selfish. And these women that he meets in London society only increase these things. They are the poison; I am the antidote.'

If Emma saw her actions as an antidote, it is questionable whether the cure was worse than the disease! Her increasing mania led Hardy to retreat into himself when alone with her at home and limit conversations to safe topics like the weather, wedding receptions or their cats.

His emotional and romantic outpourings in his literature may be as a result of this atmosphere at home. In his biography Hardy recalled his life thus: 'a triple existence unusual for a young man – what he used to call, in looking back, a life twisted of three strands – the professional life, the scholar's life, and the rustic life, combined in the twenty four hours of one day.'

Privately he shunned too personal a contact and would work hard. He was not an easy person to live with. But even in his eighties, strangely, he welcomed visitors like T.E. Lawrence, the Woolfs and Walter De La Mare to his home. While some called him witty and benign, other contemporaries thought him withdrawn, melancholy, a hermit and mean. Later Florence was to write to a friend bemoaning the small allowance for housekeeping that Hardy gave her and how she had to dip into her dress allowance to manage.

Certainly Max Gate took on the appearance of a hermitage. Before the Hardys had moved in Thomas planted trees all around the house and as they matured it was well protected from passers by.

But Hardy still loved his daily walks to escape this self-imposed prison. He and Emma had always enjoyed travelling whether by boat and train or by the humble bicycle. Hardy loved to cycle and once wrote to Emma from London in 1896: 'I have seen the loveliest "Byke" for myself – would suit me admirably – The Rover Cob. It is £20! I can't tell if I ought to have it.' When Hardy wrote this he was 56. He reacted in a similar way to the coming of the motor car, and such was the extent of his travel during his life, to Switzerland, Italy, most of southern England and certainly around his beloved Dorset, often making notes for his novels, that he has been described as a true wayfarer.

Despite this international aspect to his life, Hardy reluctantly recognised that when it came to writing he was best suited to concentrating on the environment he knew the best – the Westcountry. If the critics would not allow him to set his novels in more exotic places then he would become a mental traveller, and created Wessex.

Perhaps it is this marvellous evocation of an era long since passed that gives his writing its charisma, its fascination, indeed its magic. At the time his work was published, all successful novelists had their work serialised first of all in magazines.

This was a great advantage over authors of previous eras like Jane Austen. More and more people were learning to read with the advent of a better standard of living for more of the general population and magazines were easily accessible outside of London with improved transport. In fact the railway came to Dorchester in 1847, just seven years after Hardy was born.

The drawback to having work serialised however, was that the writer had to produce what his editor would publish and Hardy ran a constant battle over what were described at the time as the more 'shocking' elements in his novels. Any frank treatment of sex or religion was definitely taboo! When he was asked to cut out bits of *Tess of the D'Urbervilles* Hardy wrote an essay commenting that the bulk of English fiction was characterized by its lack of sincerity. After the serialisation however, the novels were published in full and they too caused a storm. Hardy seemed to be pushing back the literary frontiers creating an excitement within his audience. Who was this man, they asked, who could create characters and reveal thoughts and feelings as if they were his own?

Hardy's Wessex was in fact an area which covered not only Dorset but parts of Devon, Somerset and Hampshire. Most of the maps of the area also include a small map of Cornwall which he renamed Lyonesse and though some of the names were changed by him Hardy's Wessex can still be travelled today.

Although it may seem an insult to say that little has changed in the county and there will be many who can stand up and point out a myriad of changes, even in Hardy's day the county seemed to be very different to those around it, with its own language, culture and traditions. The heaths that Hardy so loved may be diminished in size but the panoramic views from a hilltop can still be breathtakingly beautiful. In his description of the Vale of Blackmoor in *Tess* we can still see a view very similar to this today.

'This fertile and sheltered tract of country, in which the fields are never brown and the springs never dry, is bounded on the south by the bold chalk ridge that embraces the prominences of Hambledon Hill, Bulbarrow, Nettlecombe-Tout, Dogbury, High Stoy, and Bubb Down. The traveller from the coast . . . is surprised and delighted to behold, extended like a map beneath him, a country differing absolutely from that which has passed through . . .

'Here, in the valley, the world seems to be constructed upon a smaller and more delicate scale; the fields are mere paddocks, so reduced from this height their hedgerows appear a network of dark

Gold Hill, Shaftesbury, seems to make time stand still.

Very much a part of Hardy's Dorset – the sea.

green threads over-spreading the paler green of the grass. The atmosphere beneath is langorous, and is so tinged with azure that what artists call the middle distance partakes also of that hue, while the horizon beyond is of the deepest ultramarine.'

Later, in the general preface to the novels and poems Hardy wrote about the geographical limitations he had set himself: '. . . were not absolutely forced on the writer by circumstances; he forced them upon himself by judgement . . . found sufficient room for a large proportion of its action in an extent of their county . . . here reunited under the old name of Wessex, and that the domestic emotions have throbbed in Wessex nooks with as much intensity as in the palaces of Europe, and that, anyhow, there was quite enough human nature in Wessex for one man's literary purpose.'

Incorporating dialect of any kind can be difficult for even the most skilful novelist but Hardy lovingly uses the phrases which he himself was sad to see die out in common usage. He did not agree that a dialect was vulgar even if it might give away one's humble origins. Hardy was a man who fervently believed in the immeasurable value of each human being no matter where he or she came from. His concern was with the potentiality of man, of the cruelty of man and society, of human waste. He was a champion of the individual. His attitude to dialect in his writings thus reflects what was happening in his own life for Emma ridiculed his humble origins.

His use of dialect and his feelings on its gradual loss in the community which he still took such an active interest in is illustrated in the following passage from *The Mayor of Casterbridge:* 'The sharp reprimand was not lost upon her; and in time it came to pass that for "fay" she said "succeed", that she no longer spoke of "dumbledores" but of "bumblebees"; no longer said of young men and women that they "walked together", but that they were "engaged"; that she grew to

The stunning natural rock arch at Durdle Door.

Bockhampton Church

talk of "greggles" as "wild hyacinths"; that when she had not slept she did not quaintly tell the servants next morning that she had been "hag-rid", but that she had "suffered from indigestion".'

Hardy husbanded his genius and in the same way he kept his innermost feelings to himself. Through his literature we can only surmise what he himself felt. From his letters to Emma there is a clue to the atmosphere in which he spent a goodly proportion of his life while Florence provides the few details of his final years. He seems a man of contradiction, his complexity is his mystery, his magic comes from deep within his heart, the source of his inspiration. Though his ashes were buried at Poets Corner at Westminster, an accolade that would have pleased him, his heart was removed and buried here in Dorset.

He immortalised many places, both real and fictional, through his novels. Whenever we mention Hardy the first place to spring to mind is his beloved Dorset; the county of his ancestors. The greatest compliment we can give him is that through his work he breathed new life into the tradition and language of the past.

The spirit of the county of Dorset will never die. It is cocooned in the words of Thomas Hardy.

Thomas Hardy O M reads the inscription on his Dorset grave. His ashes were buried at Poets Corner at Westminster but his heart was removed and buried in Dorset.

About the author
BARNEY CAMFIELD

Barney Camfield, who lives at Exeter, is not only a frequent visitor to Dorset, he has a deep affinity with the county – and often lectures at Sherborne and Bryanston on the Universities and Schools Network. In this chapter he explores the Arthurian connection with Dorset and uses psycho-expansion which is a form of time travel.

Barney – christened Bernard Jesse Oliver – Camfield was born at Barters Farm, eight miles south of Salisbury and has always retained a love of farming and country life. After service in the commandos during the second world war, he was invalided out in 1945 and became involved in earning his living in films and television. After a study of psychology, though, this has been his primary interest and he has become well-known for his work in the field of psychosomatic medicine and 'healing'.

Mr Camfield has been minister of Moreton-hampstead Unitarian Church since 1967, is Chairman of the Westcountry Natural Healing Fellowship and founded the Moreton Healing Fellowship with branches in the South and West.

Barney Camfield.

Arthur in Dorset

by Barney Camfield

Gereint thought of the old days as he sat astride the mount which Arthur had given him. They were moving unhurriedly along the dry bed of the winter burn. Dry because it was early summer; it took the winter rain to make it flow strongly.

Now Arthur was dead and Gereint carried in a pack a bowl to give to Arthur's heir – if he could find one. If not he would give it into the hands of those of the Old Religion. He certainly didn't want the Christians to have it. He didn't trust them still, although he had been taught at the monastery on St Michael's Island at the mouth of the Tamar.

His mind wandered back to the time he had ridden on his rough but sturdy pony along this very river bed. Then he had his top men with him, all dressed in strong leather tunics and woollen trousers bound from knee to ankle. Belts and straps over shoulders and around waists supported weapons and pouches for food and other essential items. Some of them had long woollen cloaks for added protection. They also served as blankets – or were rolled across the neck of the horses in battle providing a little extra protection.

There were monks with them then. They cared for the wounded and helped prepare the warriors spiritually for battle. They wore long dark brown robes and did not usually take part in the fighting. He thought then of Merlin and grinned, remembering how, whether Merlin was in Britain or Brittany, and though supposed to be a Christian Bishop, he

70

Barney Camfield in search of Arthur.

was so often in the thick of the fighting. But then Merlin or Melanus had 'power'. And Gereint thought back to the days before a burst of understanding had made things clearer. Enlightenment had come and he knew the power within himself: spiritual power. And he knew the links between the religions – and the differences. Before that he could not understand how someone of the Old Religion could possibly have any time for these Christians.

Some miles north-east a Christian priest was performing a ceremony with wine and bread at a small settlement of monks not far from another burn – a winburn, a meadow stream. And he too thought of when he had first been initiated into these rites and the rites of the Old Religion. Merlin had played a part in his, Michael's, education too.

Gereint was not far from what is now Winterbourne Abbas – 'Abbey by the winter stream', while Michael was at Wimborne – 'Meadow stream'. They told me so.

I'll explain. For forty years I have worked in the field of psychology and what is sometimes called parapsychology. This included regression; taking people back to apparent past lives. In 1979, following a spate of TV and radio publicity, I reluctantly agreed to take on groups as a result of hundreds of people not just expressing an interest but a strong desire to take part in reincarnational exploration. Within months we had discovered a couple of dozen who were apparently with Arturus – Dux Bellorum – the War Duke of the Britons or King Arthur as he is more familiarly known. Now we have nearly forty 'Arthurians' – not that we have made a fetish of going into the Arthurian years. We have roamed through many years and indeed found that there were some people grouped together at other times too – including the Cathar times. And religion played a large part in some of those years.

Now you can disbelieve me and throw it all, or some of it, overboard if you wish. We have checked and checked in many ways the accuracy of the findings of these people – not just in regression – the principals in particular, and have found them extremely accurate so I am inclined to accept what they tell me about the Arthurian age. The principals include Arturus, Morgana, Gereint and others who are recognisable in the stories of Arthur. But they, at this moment, do not want to be named, apart from Morgana who has been named. The BBC contacted me some time back and she was on the Russell Harty Show with Shirley Maclaine and told something of her life as Morgana. But she was the only one.

Arthur, who has been revealed in other books published by Bossiney Books as 'a brown eyed housewife', is writing a book on her life as Arthur. Gereint is a teacher in this life while Michael is a farmer. Gordon – not his real name – is another who, while having worked with us in psycho-expansion which is the technique we use in our regression exercises, is an ex RAF jet pilot. He came along with us when, with Arthur, we looked for and found his birthplace and where he was buried. And an excellent navigator he was too.

I made a number of trips to the mystical Arthurian sites with those I will call by their old names in this chapter. In each case we came first to the Nine Stones half a mile west of Winterbourne Abbas. And what a reputation they have! The Nine Ladies, The Devil's Ninestones. A man from Martinstown said the stones were the Devil, his wife and children. Another story was that they were children turned to stone for playing fivestones on a Sunday. Another tale is that they were maidens turned to stone for dancing on a Sunday.

'Although situated right beside the A35' said Michael, 'they were difficult to find as they are almost buried – and certainly surrounded by trees in a small copse. Ignoring the trees and the iron railings which sadly surround the stones – the ring itself has presence. One can feel that it is a site of mystical worship far back into antiquity. On my first visit in this life I felt that Melanus (Merlin) and Michael and his troop visited the site every time they were in the vicinity. It was a special centre for spiritual upliftment and was a must whenever possible.'

Michael psychically looked for Arthur and saw him there as a small boy of four or five, brought there by his mother and father with Melanus and others to observe a ceremony. Michael said that he felt young himself. On another occasion when I brought Arthur he found himself there, aged about four, curly haired just as Michael had described him to me. Arthur said that Michael was there aged about twelve. Arthur felt that he went there very seldom after that.

Gereint saw a young Arthur there too. And a ceremony which he felt was thanksgiving and blessing; healing. Later he drew my attention to Francis Hitching's book *Earth Magic* published by Picador in which he points out that the ritual circular movement was connected with the sun's movement and that three times three was a powerful number. Such ceremonies were performed to bring healing and blessings.

Bringing the mystical and spiritual side up to date; at 9.15 in the evening of January 23, 1985 a breakdown van towing – but not linked electrically to – a damaged Ford transit was passing the stones when its engine cut out and the lights of both vehicles died. A few moments later the electrical circuits came to life again. And guess what? UFOs have been seen in the vicinity! It does seem that the Nine Stones at Winterbourne Abbas could indeed be a spiritual – psychic 'power point'.

Could this be Arthur's birthplace?

Not so far from Winterbourne Abbas is Maiden Castle just two miles south west of Dorchester, a hill fort dating back to about 2000 BC. A defended town really. There is evidence that before the Romans invaded in 43 AD the Veneti tribe, who originally moved over from Brittany 100 years before and who were experts in sling shot warfare, had made it one of the strongest forts in Britain. Even though the Romans may not have conquered the fort itself they soon held the surrounding countryside and the hilltop dwellers left their huts to settle in Durnovaria now called Dorchester.

How Maiden Castle got its name has been hotly debated! Some say it is because 'it was never forced or won'. Others: 'where maidens found refuge in war'. One writer commented that while the Nine Maidens in Cornwall is easily understood as deriving from the Cornish maen for stone, another English explanation must be sought here. But why? There may well have been Sarsen stones there at some time. The remains of a Roman Temple and a Priest's House have been found dating from 380 AD when Christianity was the official Roman religion, but bronze figures of Pagan Gods were also found which may have been Roman or earlier. There was bound to have been some place of worship probably with standing stones at some time on the site. In any case the Veneti certainly defended well with stone. And the language was Celtic. So why not from maen?

'When Gereint was chief of the Dumnoniae, Arthur asked him to travel to his main camp in Dorset using the coast road and meeting tribal chiefs along the way,' said Gereint. 'He travelled to Isca (Exeter) and then along the coastal road – now Bridport – and then followed the dry course of the Winterbourne river. En route he met the Piscae – fisher tribe – whose lands formed the coastal defence against the Saxons as far as Weymouth. Arthur anticipated trouble here and Gereint was able to help the people prepare defensive tactics from his experiences of defending the northern coast from attack across the Severn. Another tribe along here were the Atrebates led by one Tostig with whom he became friends.

'Gereint then travelled south of and around Durnovaria, stopping at Maiden Castle for talks with Arthur and his chiefs. In spite of the Romans' use of the temple for both Pagan and Christian worship here, Arthur's visit was purely practical. He wished to assess the feasibility, should the need arise, of using the earthworks as a last defence against the Saxons. He met his chiefs here in secret as the local people were superstitious of the area. He then left to go further north and in fact this defence was never used even after Arthur's death.'

Not far away in Dorchester is Maumbury Rings; now a park. Arthur did not use this as it had been spoilt by the Romans who had changed its structure to make an amphitheatre where, as well as other gladiatorial contests, they held fist fights; their fists covered with metal studded gloves. No Queensbury rules there. The word Dorchester is derived from Celtic words meaning 'The Roman military station of the Fist Fights'. And Dorset from Durnsaete – 'The settlers around the fist fighting place'.

It is lovely now. But if you are a sensitive you may pick up a few nasty impressions. There was a gallows there until 1766 and Mary Channings, a murderess was burned in the centre while it is said 10,000 people watched. While he was there with me a little while ago Gereint looked back and keyed into Roman times and their entertainment which made him a bit sick. But it was obviously not affecting the youngsters who were enjoying a game of football there.

In this life Arthur had never been to Dorset to attempt to find where he thought he was born or to find other sites important in those earlier days. So I went to Plymouth where we spent some hours looking around with inner eyes and also at present day maps. One thing that resulted was that Arthur felt the importance of what turned out to be a triangle with the apex around Monkton-up-Wimborne, the other two points being roughly between Wimborne Minster and Blandford Forum way. I spent a day with Michael going around the triangle and also to the Nine Stones and another day with Michael, Gordon and Arthur to the triangle which Arthur had said before was powerful. And we found where Arthur was sure he was born and was buried.

The Romans defeated the local tribes at Badbury Rings, the Iron Age hillfort between Blandford and Wimborne. They had set up base camp near what is now Wimborne where a settlement sprang up and where Michael saw himself in later life celebrating communion with a dozen or so other monks. The building they were in would now cover part of the graveyard of the minster in the south east corner, over what is now King Street, the old Tudor house, St Joseph's and the very modern Methodist Church. This was a Christian ceremony and blood red wine was being used. Gereint confirmed that he too saw the religious settlement on that site.

The ceremony Michael saw at Knowlton circle, a sacred circle in which stands the ruins of a Norman church, five and a half miles north of Wimborne, was different. 'The ceremony taking place was of Druidic origin and was spoken in Gaelic. I saw a large sword lying on a sacred stone and the ritual of the blessing of the sword included four small objects – dishes – being placed carefully on the stone around the sword. They may have contained, symbolically, the four elements. Each chieftain and about six of his most loyal men went forward individually to have their own personal sword blessed and empowered. After it had been endowed with power each warrior knelt and was dubbed quite heavily on each shoulder which also recharged him and gave him great self-confidence. He kissed the blade near the hilt and returned to his place with his recharged sword. It occurred to me that the four elements, air, water, earth and fire were required and used in the making of the sword.

'Gereint saw the swords being blessed when they were made. Fire, water, earth and the 'wind of the spirit' were used in the manufacture. At the ceremony seen by Michael, and later by Gereint, fire, water and earth powers were withdrawn increasing the power of the spirit for battle,' said Gereint.

Michael said of the circle: 'It is a special, mystical, highly powered area. On my first visit it excited and enthralled me. It was definitely a site that was revered; a meeting place. Melanus was very much the Bishop there, conducting a service for spiritual strength and upliftment. The leaders of the tribes came to get recharged as it were; it was an occasion where they took second place before Melanus and Michael and the small group of monks. They accepted the spiritual authority here – but not always elsewhere. This was a sacred area reserved for the chiefs and the main ceremonies. Not for the common man; it was too strong and powerful for his comprehension.' Perhaps it still is.

'I saw another service or ceremony on my second visit. Melanus was speaking, in Latin I think, and his monks were grouped around him in a semi-circle. The chieftains were sprawled in front of him – slightly sheepish, slightly reluctant, slightly adverse, slightly defiant, but knowing that they needed the recharging Melanus could give them. And his advice and admonishments. Their sprawling I think was their outward gesture of independence and non-conformity.'

Gordon said that there was a good feeling here and that leaving the circle he felt heavy. Some are wary of the place because they say that modern day witches have been sacrificing frogs and the like in

Knowlton, a sacred circle in which stands the ruins of a Norman church.

the church. If they have done so they have not much power because none of us felt anything but good there. Even a visitor from Wimborne with his little boy said that it felt good though sometimes places felt 'anything but' to him – even some churches.

Here Arthur too was at home. And visibly energised. He strode today as the Arthur of yesteryear, not with the gait of present life. He said he felt so lifted and had certainly been here with the Chiefs. He could see himself at the top of a wooden tower scanning the distant hills and waiting, waiting. Battles had been fought near here. A successful one at Spetisbury Rings, a hillfort a couple of miles from Badbury Rings. Mention of the latter made Arthur irritated. 'Not of importance!' But Knowlton was. It was a powerful centre still having lots of energy. Arthur used this both as a rallying point and a centre for religious services. Here the swords and other arms were dedicated and the chiefs received their spiritual power.

And the surrounding area. Monkton-up-Wimborne was a holy site of the uprising of the waters. Power and strength came from there too. And Wimborne St Giles just a mile or two away where there is a beautiful church with a lovely feeling. There have been well established settlements here for several thousand years. And who knows how many of Arthur's men lie buried in the huge cemetery – a number of large barrows still remain between here and Knowlton Circle. Arthur said that at Wimborne St Giles he, as Dux Bellorum, would visit, for advice, a wise man whom he believed was a relative.

Gordon's navigation and our psychical noses – especially Arthur's of course – led us to the birthplace of Arthur who had also told me that he had been brought back to the place of his birth to be buried. In *Strange Somerset Stories* published by Bossiney Books in 1984 he was quoted as saying that he believed that Arthur was born in Dorset and on page 100 says that after his death they carried him '... through an old valley and the place is heavily wooded with the most enormous trees, and the clue ... ah! ... follow the ley line from Glastonbury south west, that will find the area, and there are still woods along this path now, but no little consequence to ask what town they were at.

'There is an older encampment or it was there. It is marked now on a map as a castle or fortress, set on a crag within this forest. And there is a hidden place within, they are like caves, and it is approached by a path going around the crag. There was a trench built, it is a ditch and it has not been in use, and it is an old fortress even in their time – the time I am dealing with now. It is in disuse so it is only known to a few this place, and they are going along following the ditch outline, then coming right along the crag as it were. Remember that there are trees all over, overshadowing this whole thing. The trees are in leaf, denoting the time of year for Arthur's death, and it is an extraordinary place.

'There are caves, a series of them, but there is a biggish entrance which is not quite on top. It is underneath the rock, but there is an opening – a portion open to the sky. There is an area in front of this cave entrance which is cleared and there is a stone, a standing stone there. Is it still there now? If it is still there, if it is, it's lost in all the undergrowth or whatever and that stone is in line with Glastonbury. It isn't a huge stone – it doesn't have to be because of the height of the promontory. That's where they are. It almost seems as though it is on the borders of Somerset and Dorset.'

Following the trail across Dorset.

'That's where I'm buried' said Arthur.

We had been around Cerne Abbas and had gone on to Minterne Magna two miles north. It was nearby that Arthur had been born, in a wooden house now long gone. But immediately after birth he had been taken to the spring, yards away, for his 'blessing'. His mother was a beautiful golden haired woman. She was of Romano-British descent – as were many of the chiefs and others of the aristocracy of the day – hence their knowledge of Latin kept up by the Christian priests of course. She had come to a safe area to be with a relative – maybe a sister – and there she delivered Aries born Arthur.

We had found where the spring had then sprung, in a copse. If you look where the four roads meet, travelling north on the A352 half a mile or so from Minterne Magna and a couple of yards up on the right of the right hand road – which says it is unfit for motor vehicles – you'll find some stone steps – Victorian I would say – up the bank into a triangular copse (OS Sheet 104; 657/053). There indeed are the earthworks. And look to your left as Arthur did that afternoon and you'll see a hill close by. 'It's there. That's where I'm buried,' said he.

*   *   *

Geraint thought of the bowl in the pack slung across his horse. He looked up at the three figures carved into the hillside, the woman and the king flanking the rampant, club wielding giant in the middle. It had been said that it was because Arthur had seen this figure so often when young that it had inspired him to father so many children. But Gereint could not find an heir. 'Arthur sleeps at Avalon' he had been told. He smiled to himself and set off for Avalon.

About the author
FELICITY YOUNG

Felicity Young is a Cornish-based painter who lives at Tintagel. In 1987 she did twenty especially commissioned drawings for Bossiney's first two Dorset titles. Since 1984, she has drawn more than 150 illustrations for the Westcountry publishers. A water colourist, many of her paintings grow from sketches, notes and photographs on location.

Educated at Lord Digby's Grammar School, Sherborne, Felicity says: 'Dorset is a county so full of legend that the artist's imagination is easily fired by tales of ghostly happenings and by the intriguing characters who have lived here. You cannot fail to be affected by the sense of mystery which surrounds the beautiful landscape.' This is her debut as a Bossiney author.

Felicity Young

Lawrence of Arabia

By Felicity Young

Who would have believed that Dorset, this most English of counties, and Arabia, a land of vast desert and bare rock, could possibly have something in common?

But there is a link, albeit a curious one in the person of T E Lawrence, who remains to this day a Dorset mystery. He is buried in an annexe of the churchyard at Moreton and a beautiful carved effigy of Lawrence in Arab dress adorns a tomb in St Martin's Church, Wareham. He remains as much a part of Dorset folklore as he does its history and the mysterious circumstances surrounding his death have given him a place among the many strange and intriguing stories which abound in this beautiful county.

T E Lawrence was born in Tremadoc in Caernarvonshire, North Wales on August 15, 1888, a date of which he was especially proud since it was the birthday of Napoleon Bonaparte, who had been born in 1769. He seems to have been a man born with a mission. Even though he came from a large family, the second of five sons, he was very much a loner. From early childhood he had become interested in archaeology, particularly medieval and Roman art. The theme of the Crusades caught his imagination and it seems ironic that this dream of freeing a race from bondage should finally become a reality when he took up the Arab campaign some years later.

Lawrence was an enigma, a poet and a scholar, remaining a lone figure for most of his life. He found his schooldays tiresome, the restrictions imposed upon him interfered very much with his private studies, in contrast he enjoyed the freedom offered at university.

It was during his schooldays that he acquired his taste for speed.

He cycled everywhere at great speed, pushing himself to the limit, testing his endurance and striving to achieve the utmost from man and machine. He had, apparently, been the first at his school to own a three-speed, drop-handlebar racing bicycle and he made many ambitious rides to Wales and even France on it. At university he gained something of a reputation for devising almost impossible challenges which he would undertake alone, such as the night time navigation of an underground stream in Oxford. He had discovered it in the works of a seventeenth century historian and he felt obliged to verify its existence. He also tried at one time to see how long he could survive without food or sleep, he had managed 45 hours when he finally burst into the room of a fellow student, brandishing a revolver, in a very disturbed state.

Lawrence chose to read at Oxford University 'The Influence of the Crusaders on Medieval Military Architecture of Europe' and to help with these studies he decided to visit alone on foot, the castles of the Crusades in Syria.

It was there in Syria that he began to pick up the Arabic language from the villagers and Sheiks with whom he stayed on his journey. He narrowly escaped murder and was struck down with malaria but he came through his adventures with the feeling of being drawn like a magnet to the Bedouin way of life; the desert was already in his blood. He was obviously a man who enjoyed a challenge especially one which entailed a certain amount of danger. So began a new chapter in his life, following the direction in which fate was drawing him so strongly, ever nearer his role as 'The Uncrowned Prince of Arabia'.

Having finished his thesis he returned to Syria with the British Museum expedition to the Upper Euphrates. And during this time his friendship with a young boy nicknamed Dahoum – little dark one – helped Lawrence cross the divide between his western background and the eastern way of life.

Dahoum accompanied him on many expeditions exploring the vast countryside and Lawrence frequently adopted Arab clothing to be like his companion; this mode of dress became something of a trademark later on. The Arabs working on the site with Lawrence did not approve of the friendship with Dahoum and when Lawrence carved the naked, crouching figure of his friend out of local limestone and set it up on the edge of his house they were even more horrified, fearing some evil spirit was afoot.

In the summer of 1913 Lawrence brought Dahoum, and another

rather wild character with whom he had become close friends, Sheik Hamoudi, home with him to Oxford. They created a sensation in the town, much to Lawrence's amusement, by cycling around on ladies' bicycles in their flowing Arab robes.

It was while he was working with the British Museum expedition that Lawrence first caught the eye of the press. There were rumours that the expedition was in fact a spying mission which Lawrence dismissed as nonsense. But suggestions like these would become all too familiar later when almost everything he did was speculated about and evaluated as undercover work or spying. And it was this, perhaps more than anything, which ultimately led to his finding his Dorset retreat, the beautiful whitewashed cottage, Clouds Hill, where he could find refuge from the public.

But having denied spying allegations Lawrence soon found himself in a different position. He was invited to join the Royal Engineers in a geographical survey to draw up military maps. The survey had been instigated by Kitchener and to give the whole business plausible cover the operation was under the auspices of a respectable archaeological organisation. Lawrence wrote to his mother on the subject saying that he thought they were obviously there '... as red herrings to give archaeological colour to a political job'. Of course this only added fuel to the propaganda fire later on.

During the Arab campaigns which followed, Lawrence made promises to his friend, Emir Faseil on behalf of Britain that freedom of the Arab people from German and Turkish domination would lead to a unified country for the Arabs. But without his knowledge the Allies made a secret agreement that large areas of the territories of the Ottoman Empire would be partitioned off, greatly to Faseil's disadvantage. When Lawrence learned of this he suffered a great moral dilemma. He had gained Faseil's support in the war under false pretences and he felt guilt and remorse which remained with him throughout his life. When the French Liaison Officer came to Faseil to offer guidance in the protection of Syria, Faseil refused to have anything to do with him. Lawrence, feeling that he had let Faseil down, also refused to work with the French and requested to be sent home to England; so another chapter in his life came to a close, T E Lawrence's part in the Arab Campaign was over.

Once back home in England he took up life as an 'ordinary' man in the ranks of the RAF under the pseudonym, firstly of Ross, then later as Shaw and he again found great comfort in speed this time on a motorcycle. For him it brought some kind of release, he was so obsessed with speed that he obtained one of the fastest, most powerful motorcycles of the day, a Brough Superior, apparently a present from his friends Mr and Mrs Bernard Shaw. He would cover up to 600 miles some weeks, his love of motorcycling never seemed to diminish.

Just as he had gained a reputation in his youth for his cycling achievements, now he gained a reputation for his reckless desire for speed on his motorcycle, in whatever he did he never went unnoticed. Lawrence would find some kind of freedom, reaching speeds of 100 miles an hour, racing through the winding roads of Dorset, travelling to and from London, over undulating hills along narrow lanes, perhaps at greater speeds than were safe. The danger spurred him on as though he had a death wish, he wanted to risk his life, wanted to die to free himself from his conscience. It was another quirk of fate that his great love of motorcycling should finally be instrumental in his death.

Even as aircraftman Shaw in the RAF where he had hoped to find anonymity the press found him and caused a sensation with a story about Lawrence 'The arch spy of the world', incognito participating in a secret mission in Afghanistan. He continued to be hounded by the press, they even followed him to Clouds Hill his only real sanctuary. Several times in the last few weeks before his death he had been driven away from his cottage by cameramen and reporters clamouring for a story.

Lawrence had found the cottage derelict and quite secluded among trees, close to Bovington Camp. He set about gradually restoring and furnishing it with money earned from his writings and with cash raised from the sale of a gold dagger from Mecca. He once wrote of his own little Mecca, describing it in these words '... the cottage is alone in a dip in the moor, very quiet, very lonely, very bare. A mile from camp. Furnished with a bed, a bicycle, three chairs, 100 books, a gramophone of parts, a table ... no food, except what a grocer and the camp shops and canteens provide; milk, wood fuel for the picking up. I don't sleep here, but come out at 4.30pm until 9pm nearly every evening, and dream, or write or read by the fire, or play Beethoven or Mozart to myself.'

He often invited his friends, John Galsworthy, E M Forster, Thomas Hardy and Lady Astor to name but a few, to eat food out of tins and relax and enjoy the peaceful atmosphere. The Hardys owned

Clouds Hill – Lawrence's retreat from the world. He found the cottage derelict and gradually restored and furnished it with money earned from his writings.

a little terrier, called Wessex, which apparently had a ferocious temperament, not abashed by the collection of celebrities, poets, authors and even a famous surgeon, it would tear any trouser leg to ribbons. The only person to escape by some strange magic it seemed was Lawrence.

On the morning of his accident, Tuesday May 13, 1935, Lawrence was travelling along the road to Bovington Camp from Clouds Hill, a road he knew well, when he swerved to avoid two errand boys cycling along. He touched one of the boys' bicycle wheels and his Brough went out of control throwing him onto the road. He did not die instantly but remained in a coma in hospital for six days before he

Nancy Astor, the much loved Plymouth Member of Parliament, was a
frequent vistor at Clouds Hill.

died. There was as much speculation surrounding his death as there had been during his lifetime, there was even talk of conspiracy and murder. It came to light that he had been asked by his friend Henry Williamson, author and supporter of the British Fascist Movement, in a letter to Lawrence – a letter which incidentally has never been found – to meet with Adolf Hitler. Williamson felt that Hitler would be greatly influenced by such a man as Lawrence. It had been arranged that he would meet Williamson the next day and he was on his way to send a telegram when the fatal accident occurred.

The mystery of T E Lawrence's death has lingered on to this day, perhaps it was all speculation and he simply was not concentrating on that clear, bright May morning. His mind may have been occupied with thoughts concerning the telegram to his friend and the relevance of the forthcoming meeting. He had been known to say that he would do anything to avoid running over even a hen. Although to swerve on a motorcycle was a great risk it was a greater risk to actually hit something, so he probably acted instinctively to avoid the two errand boys on their bicycles. Or was it some kind of plot to halt the career of a brilliant man before he could cast his influence over some threatening power, completely altering the outcome of world events. He most probably would have played an important role in the forthcoming world war, had he lived, considering his close friendship

Winston Churchill – a man who admired Lawrence greatly.

93

with Winston Churchill, a man who admired Lawrence greatly. Undoubtedly he would have answered his call in the face of a national emergency. Or was he just a great man born with one mission and one mission only, to play the part of crusader as he himself had dreamed, and that achieved to quietly slip away.

The fact that there have been strange stories which began shortly after his death, about a ghostly form in Arab dress seen entering Clouds Hill, a figure which for no apparent reason disappears once inside, makes one wonder whether even in death he was still a restless, unquiet figure searching for the peace he had not been able to find in life, seeking eternal solace in his cottage. He had written a message to Lady Astor on one of his personalised cards only five days before he died, which read 'Wild mares would not at present take me away from Clouds Hill. It is an earthly paradise.' He obviously had no intention of leaving his home at that time, indeed he was still in the process of renovating the cottage making it a fit place for him to spend the rest of his days.

He was in a sombre mood just before his death, almost a broken man who needed to recover from the pressure heaped upon him by the constant attention of the press. He expressed his feelings in his last notes and letters to his friends saying how empty he felt 'something has gone dead inside me now' and 'I am a leaf fallen from its tree.' His death may have been caused by outside influences or perhaps fate had planned that at last he could be happy, taking up refuge in his cottage in a ghostly form, undisturbed at last, allowed to come and go as he pleased, drifting in and out at will, unhindered by reality, unencumbered by a material body.

The enigma of the man has continued throughout history. He had many close friends, famous authors, academics and politicians but still he was able to take on the role of an 'ordinary' man in the RAF and Tank Corps in later life. He saw himself as classless, he felt his upbringing, adventures and way of thinking had bereft him of class, making him every man's equal. He was fuelled by a vision of a united Arabia, a dream of fame and romance, but when finally it came to him he tried desperately to shun it, always trying to escape the limelight and fade into obscurity. Unfortunately a man of such achievement and obvious genius would find it hard to escape from public attention for long. His conquests in the Arab campaigns and his engimatic life meant people were naturally curious, he had become a national hero and as such he was not allowed any privacy. The pressures may have

The stretch of road where Lawrence lost control of his Brough Superior motorcycle with fatal consequences.

been responsible for pushing him nearer and nearer to the edge that he often came close to on his motorcycle until finally one day he went beyond his limits and lost control of his machine with fatal consequences. The two errand boys have never been traced, if indeed they ever existed at all, perhaps they were not considered relevant at the time. Maybe the most important thing was that the tormented man who had been labelled 'The Uncrowned Prince of Arabia' had finally found peace.

MORE BOSSINEY BOOKS . . .

STRANGE DORSET STORIES
introduced by David Foot

Six authors – and their publisher – probe strange aspects of Dorset. David Foot in his scene-setting first chapter says 'The history of the county reverberates intriguingly with the varied whims of strange people . . . and strange happenings.'

UNKNOWN DORSET
by Alison Poole and Michael Williams

An exploration of the off-the-beaten-track places. Many especially commissioned illustrations.

LEGENDS OF DORSET
by Polly Lloyd

The author explores legendary Dorset, visiting places as diverse as the Sacred Circle at Knowlton and Chesil Beach. Dorset is a mine of myth and folklore.

'Weird happenings . . . Polly Lloyd delves through tales ranging from moving rocks to murders . . .'
Ed Perkins, Southern Evening Echo

GHOSTS OF DORSET
by Peter Underwood

The President of the Ghost Club explores a whole range of Dorset hauntings. A ghostly white donkey, a world-famous screaming skull, phantom coach-and-horses story which Thomas Hardy used in *Tess of the D'Ubervilles* and a prehistoric 'Peeping Tom' are some of the subjects.

'Ghost hunter Peter Underwood has been spook stalking in Dorset uncovering a host of eerie brushes with the Supernatural.'

Bournemouth Advertiser

MYSTERIOUS PLACES
by Peter Underwood

Visits locations that 'seem to have been touched by a magic hand'. The man who has been called Britain's No. 1 ghost hunter reflects: 'We live in a very mysterious world . . .'

'. . . an insight into some of the more mysterious places in the south west.'
Davis Elvidge, Launceston & Bude Gazette

We shall be pleased to send you our catalogue giving full details of our growing list of titles for Devon, Cornwall, Dorset, Somerset and Wiltshire and forthcoming publications. If you have difficulty in obtaining our titles, write direct to Bossiney Books, Land's End, St. Teath, Bodmin, Cornwall.